SENIOR SELLING

Focusing on
The Greatest Generation
of Savers This Country
Has Ever Known

By

Anthony Raad

Any reference to places, events, and/or situations in this book are meant to be a symbolic and collective reference to specific experiences in the author's business. Any part of this book taken alone is not a specific reference to any one person or event. Any resemblance to actual persons, living or dead, is unintentional and merely coincidental.

ISBN: 1-4107-3847-7 (e-book)
ISBN: 1-4107-3846-9 (Paperback)

This book is printed on acid free paper.

1stBooks - rev. 05/22/03

Acknowledgements

I would like to thank my broker dealer, Harbour Investments out of Madison, Wisconsin. Thanks to Harbour's hard work and meticulous attention to detail, I am able to spend my time doing what I do best. I have experienced other broker dealers during the span of my career, and Harbour has been, bar none the "cream of the crop". Harbour has provided me with excellent service and access to some of the most knowledgeable professionals in the industry.

* * * * * *

I would like to thank the staff at Financial Independence Group out of North Carolina. I have been using Financial Independence Group for years now as one of my main vendors for fixed annuity products. They always go above and beyond to provide exemplary service and to make sure I am completely satisfied. Together with their fine menu of products to offer the client, they are among the best.

Financial Independence Group Inc. is a full service brokerage firm (marketing company) based in N.C. They conduct business in 49 states and market all lines of products including annuities, LTC, and med sups. My marketer there is Phil Graham who has supported the explosive growth of my business. Phil, along with all of the marketers there has a vested interest in helping the representative grow his or her business. The staff at FIG firmly believes that they need to work hard to free up more of your time so that you can see more clients. And that is what being a marketer is about.

Thanks again to Bill, Bo, and Phil specifically, for believing that this book will increase an agent's production just by reading it and putting the ideas to work.

* * * * * *

A special thanks also goes to Allianz Life for supporting this book. I have personally been out to their home office in Minneapolis and witnessed first hand an A-1 operation firing on all cylinders. Their products fit phenomenally well within the markets I work. They continually surprise me with new and exciting products to introduce to my prospects and clients.

Allianz Life has an agent service line called the FASTeam. The FASTeam is no doubt second to none in expediting new business and taking care of my needs as a writing agent. Coupled with the producer perks program they offer, this company has been nothing but a pleasure to do business with.

* * * * * *

I would like to extend thanks to the annuity companies and their wholesalers that have supported this book. These companies include: American Skandia and GE Financial Assurance. In addition to these companies, I would also like to thank Jeff, Neil and Pauline – you know who you are.

* * * * * *

A personal thanks goes out to my creative marketing team manager Patricia Swanson, who played an important role in getting this book published.

* * * * * *

Last, but certainly not least, I would like to thank my wife Pilar for always supporting me. By temporarily forgoing her own career and staying home to raise our daughters Vanessa and Natalie, she has given me the opportunity to focus on a career I am proud of with the peace of mind knowing that our children are in the best of hands all day long.

Table of Contents

INTRODUCTION   **XI**

CHAPTER ONE   **1**

The Inspiration

CHAPTER TWO   **6**

Who Not to Prospect

CHAPTER THREE   **11**

Herein Lies the Money

CHAPTER FOUR   **16**

The Most Important Part of the Sale

CHAPTER FIVE   **21**

Let's Talk About You

CHAPTER SIX   **29**

Your Office Team is Your Office Team

CHAPTER SEVEN 34

The Pre-Game Warm-up

CHAPTER EIGHT 40

The Red Carpet is All Rolled Out

CHAPTER NINE 48

Never Judge a Book by Its Cover

CHAPTER TEN 53

Use Your Time Wisely

CHAPTER ELEVEN 58

Ask the Right Questions

CHAPTER TWELVE 63

Sit Back and Enjoy the Show

CHAPTER THIRTEEN 67

The Sole Purpose

CHAPTER FOURTEEN 71

Get the Statements

CHAPTER FIFTEEN 75

Choose Your Words Carefully

CHAPTER SIXTEEN 80

The Company

CHAPTER SEVENTEEN 85

The Product

CHAPTER EIGHTEEN 90

From Prospect to Client

CHAPTER NINETEEN 95

More Important Than the Sale

CHAPTER TWENTY 103

Have Another Drink, and Another

CHAPTER TWENTY-ONE 109

How I Knew

CHAPTER TWENTY-TWO 114

The Best Salesperson You Know

Introduction

Too many financial service representatives out there are failing in this business, day in and day out. Granted, it's an extremely difficult business, but it can also be very rewarding if things are done right. The main problem is that when things are done incorrectly, there is no one to tell you what error was committed. This book will always be available to you as a reference guide.

Formerly, during my career as a sales manager, I witnessed many salespeople who became depressed because they just couldn't close any sales. I also trained many people to be successful and had a blast doing it.

The truth of the matter here is that people who continually fail in this business probably never had a chance to close their sales to begin with. The sale was lost before they ever made it to the point of sitting around a table with the prospect to start selling. And that's exactly my point. The sales process begins long before the point of even meeting a prospect. This is precisely what this book is going to teach you.

What ultimately drove me to write this book was taking note of the increased sales I made by repeating successful habits time after time, and failures by others who repeated their mistakes over and over again. The funny part about it is that if you become better at making sales after reading this book, you might actually develop clients that I otherwise would have had. It just kills me to see so many people losing the race before they even begin to run. It's kind of like that feeling you get when someone drags their fingernails down a chalkboard. That's the feeling I get when I see another salesperson do something ridiculous, and yet never give it a second thought. I just want to smack them across the face and say, "Hey, wake up! You're making all of this way too difficult for yourself!"

The ideas that you will encounter in this book will show you how to make the sales process so simple that it will dramatically increase your closing success. There is one catch however; you must practice and make use of the ideas. If you don't apply the ideas, you will continue to make the same mistakes, and thus continue to fail at making the sale.

As you read these ideas and stories, don't try to implement everything all at once. Try little things here and there and you will see them work. Eventually though, you must make these ideas a part of your daily sales routine. They must become second nature and habitual. If I point out a certain type of person in this book and it describes you, please don't feel offended. Rather take note and change the way you are doing things. Remember, this book is your friend. It will take your sales to a new level.

This book is not meant to make personal attacks on anyone. However, it is meant to make attacks on poor sales techniques that cost you money. Again, take note and you will make more money. This book is designed to help you analyze what you are doing and what to do to correct the mistakes. The whole purpose here is to help salespeople make more money simply by using proven sales techniques. Don't continue to spend valuable time with a prospect trying to make a sale that you may have lost before you ever met them.

Chapter One

The Inspiration

During my normal prospecting telephone calls, I came across an eighty-seven-year-old gentleman, a widower, in need of my services. After a pleasant five-minute conversation, he agreed to see me. I scheduled the appointment to meet him at his home at 9:00 A.M. on a Tuesday morning.

On arriving at his home on that ninety-degree summer day, I parked my car in the street, walked up to the door, rang the doorbell and patiently waited.

1

Karl opened the door and greeted me with a smile. We proceeded to the kitchen table where we sat down and began to chat. As I looked around, the home was typical for this type of person, of this age group, in that particular part of town.

It was a nice home, however a bit unkempt and outdated. I knew within five minutes of talking to Karl that he had money. I knew within another five minutes that I would turn him from a prospect into a client. I sat and talked with Karl about the old days and listened intently to some of his memories. After about half an hour, I pulled out my palm pilot, made a follow-up appointment, exchanged a firm handshake and said goodbye.

One week later, I went back to visit with Karl again and within forty-five minutes, he signed over a $150,000 annuity which was out of the surrender period. This money was transferred and the commissions were paid to me all within a three-week period. I then went back to see Karl after I had the new annuity policy in hand to personally deliver it to him. On delivery, Karl signed over $135,000 from another annuity, which was also out of the surrender period.

During the period of time it takes for the 1035 exchange to be completed (this can take a long time to get the money from the surrendering company, as we all know), Karl received a telephone call from a young lady from ABC Life claiming to be his agent on an old $1,000 life insurance policy. She wanted to review it with him, and he invited her over for an appointment.

To make a long story short, being a lonely eighty-seven-year-old widower, yes, believe it or not, Karl was attracted to this young lady and thus told her about all the business he had been doing with me. She seized the opportunity to try to derail my sale, and I only learned about this during my normal follow-up phone call. Karl really did like me and invited me over to his home to visit with him the next time young Susie was to be there. For the first time in my twelve-year career,

I took someone up on the offer to meet another representative face to face to defend my sale.

First let me say that when I met Susie, I could see why Karl was easily swayed. She was an attractive young lady and was using her looks to her advantage in the sales process. However, before Susie arrived, I had decided to get there a bit earlier, just to try to solidify my relationship with Karl even more. Karl and I talked about everything but business for the forty-five minutes preceding the arrival of Susie. Finally Susie showed up. I was sitting at the kitchen table when the doorbell rang and Karl got up to answer the door. I remained seated since I figured, why stand up and greet someone at the door when I didn't even live there. From the kitchen, I heard the voice of a man at the front door and it wasn't Karl's voice. As you may have guessed, Susie brought her manager with her. To my surprise, it turned out that young Susie was still in training and decided it would be a good idea to bring along the big gun. At this point, I had decided to get up to see what I had gotten myself into. I had complete confidence in myself, but this had thrown a bit of a curve ball at my original plans.

As I made my way to the front room to greet the two newcomers, my eyes suddenly lit up and a sense of relief overwhelmed me. I knew instantly the sale was mine, and that it would just be a matter of going through the motions at the kitchen table. I shook hands with Susie and her manager Sylvester with a smile on my face. I was now ready to take care of business.

Within one month after that meeting, Karl proceeded to sign over another $300,000 in assets, and two things happened. Number one—I made a client for life, and number two—I made a lot of money.

The above story is true and as you read on in this book, I will be referring to it frequently to fill in the blanks about such matters as how and when I knew the sale was made; the reasons why the sale was made; and how Susie and Sylvester the Sales Manager blew the sale for themselves.

Chapter Two
Who Not to Prospect

This book isn't about making you feel good or bad about yourself. It is not about whitewashing ideas or beating around the bush. It is about telling you exactly how it really is out there in the world of sales surrounding the financial services industry. It is about you making a lot more money after you read this book and implement the ideas.

Do not, I repeat, do not spend your valuable time prospecting younger people. Let's define younger people. Younger people are those who are under the age of sixty and still working.

Generally speaking, younger people are royal pains in the you-know-what. I should know because I am a younger person. I know how my friends think. Younger people often have their money committed to everything except savings. The savings rate in this country is at a record low. Younger folks are not concerned with saving money; they are more worried about how they can spend it. For every dollar they make, they spend a buck and a quarter. However, it's not always their fault. Perhaps they are paying for their kids' college educations, which is a credible excuse, but don't make it your problem.

If you are lucky enough to come across a younger person with money, one of three things is going to happen. First, there is the outside chance that after a lot of work, you might, and I stress *might,* actually get the account. The second thing is that they may already have a broker and therefore will siphon your brain of all your information, but take it back to their brother-in-law or whoever they happen to be working with. And last, they will analyze things to death over a series of appointments, and make the actual cost of doing business for you far outweigh the potential commissions on their investment.

Also, young people cancel appointments. Trust me; bowling night with the boys is much more important to them than their financial security. It will screw up your whole schedule. Nine times out of ten, they won't even give you the courtesy of a phone call to tell you they are canceling, and you will be left wondering what happened.

Don't get me completely wrong here. I have plenty of young clients, but those prospects had to meet strict criteria before they became my client. First, they had to give me a full disclosure over the telephone as to what their assets were. Second, they had to agree over the telephone to do business with me. If these two things held true, I agreed to meet with them. Don't agree to meet with just anybody during evening hours. It must be worth your time. Set a dollar amount for yourself. For me, it's $100,000. If a younger prospect has $100,000 or more, I will forgo dinner with my wife and quality time with my children to meet the client at 6:30 P.M. to invest the money. Otherwise, the meeting must be at my office during normal business hours. Put it in simple perspective for yourself. When was the last time your doctor agreed to give you your annual physical at 7:30 P.M.? You have to take time off of work to see your doctor, because that is just the way it is. If it is important enough for you to do, you will do it. If financial security is important enough for a younger prospect, he or she will take off of work to come and see you.

There is always the 401k argument. I always hear from people, "How can you pass up all that 401k rollover money?" I don't pass it up; I just don't go out looking for it. If it comes to me, I roll it over. Don't spend time wining and dining a fifty-year-old who is going to retire in ten years, just to get that 401k rollover. Please, please, please think about it. It's just not worth it. You should be spending that time talking to other prospects who I will outline in the next chapter.

There is one exception to the above criteria. This one exception outweighs everything I have written so far in regard to young people. If a young prospect is the son or daughter of one of your "A" senior clients, you always make time to see them. However, only give them one bite at the apple, and if it's an evening appointment, take note of chapter ten to determine whether or not your efforts are going to develop into a sale or not, and how quickly you can determine when you should actually end the appointment.

Chapter Three
Herein Lies the Money

The question now arises. Who, then should we be prospecting? They answer is plain and simple—prospect seniors and only seniors. The senior population is where the money is. Seniors control trillions of dollars of wealth in the United States. Our mothers and fathers, or for some people, grandparents, are the greatest generation of savers this country has ever known. So prospect them and control their wealth with them before they die and pass the money onto the greatest generation of spenders this country has ever known.

Have you ever heard anyone ask a financial representative who their target market was? How often do you hear someone answer, "I work in the senior market?" This response always cracks me up. The fact of the matter is that most people out there know the senior market as people who are old. That's the extent of their knowledge. My question to you is—do you really want to work in the senior market? If you do, then you must understand seniors. Most people who work in that segment of the population haven't a clue. If you truly want to make more money, if you really want to understand the senior market, if you want to control your appointments rather than having them control you, then read on. If you think you have it all figured out, you can put this book down right now.

Let's define a senior prospect. Let's also keep it very simple. A senior prospect is anyone over the age of sixty and retired. These are the people you should be talking to on a daily basis. These are the people who are worthy of your time.

Look at the lifestyle of a typical senior. Their kids are out of school. Their cars are almost certainly paid for in cash. Their homes are completely paid off. They actually have money saved in CDs, money markets and bank savings accounts. These people are flush with money, and aching for someone to tell them what to do with it. They aren't over-analyzers, and typically, they don't like to deal with other family members when it comes to their money—unlike younger people, for whatever reason. Their brother's, sister's, aunt's, daughter's goldfish is a financial planner, accountant or a lawyer who they have to get a second opinion from before they invest. The senior prospect is usually the sole decision maker.

Generally speaking, seniors don't cancel appointments. These people have a whole different philosophy ground into them. When they make an appointment, they respect it and keep it. Let me prove this to you. For those of you who have senior clients, when trying to schedule an appointment with them, have you ever encountered any of the following objections?

"Oh, I'm sorry, Tuesday won't work for me. I have a doctor's appointment that day."

"Oh, I'm sorry; we can't see you on Monday. That's our shopping day."

"Thursday—nope that's out. Mildred does laundry on Thursdays."

These are committed people. I have never in my life been to a doctor's appointment that has taken up the whole day, and I don't know about you, but my washing machine has a forty-five minute timed cycle on it. Once a senior commits to something, it's all or nothing. They don't change their minds; they don't cancel appointments; and they have all the money. What more could you ask for? Glad I asked that question, because the real kicker here is that they are all daytime appointments!

There are a couple of catches to having these perfect people as your clients. First of all, a prospect is only a prospect and not a source of income until you turn them into a client. You *must* first turn them into a client. The second catch is that maintaining them as clients doesn't mean that the deal is closed after they sign on the dotted line. There is much more to it than that. You want these people long-term. Remember, they are the best generation of savers in the history of this country, and just because you've gotten them to invest their money with you, it doesn't mean they suddenly will quit saving on that very day. These clients can be a continual source of income for you. By understanding the senior psyche, you can keep drinking from the same well over and over again.

Chapter Four

The Most Important Part of the Sale

Before you sell anything to anyone—I don't care what the product is—you must first understand the natural order of things. You have to ingrain in your mind what I am about to tell you right now. When people *do* buy something, they are buying from you first, the company second, and the product third. This is Sales 101. I am sure most of you have heard this before, but the fact of the matter is you don't practice it. Say it over and over again in your head a thousand times until you believe it.

Before I go into the "you" portion of this chapter, I want to prove that people buy from you first. Let me give an example. Where do you go to buy a new lawn mower? The answer is quite simple. You go to a reputable, local hardware store, or in my situation, I'd prefer Home Depot. Either one fits this example just fine. The Home Depot in this example describes "you."

After you get to Home Depot, what do you do? You go to the area where the lawn mowers are sold and you are instantly attracted to the brand names. Some popular brand names are Toro, Lawn Boy, and Simplicity, just to name a few. This brand name represents the "company." You rarely even look at something unless it has a name you recognize.

After you have kicked a few tires or moved a few levers up and down, you start to read the manual to figure out all the goodies that come with this lawn mower. This part describes the "product."

17

Think about it; did I just describe that perfectly or what? Now think of some other examples in your head. It always works the same way. I will say it again: you first, the company second and the product third.

Now let's examine an example of something most of us wouldn't even think of purchasing. When you go to the grocery store, what do you buy? Of course, the answer is groceries. I love walking around the grocery store, especially when I am hungry. Everything looks so good. I have even opened things up and eaten them as I shopped, only to hand the cashier an empty wrapper to ring up at the register as I am checking out. I can't tell you how many times I have gone into my favorite grocery store, and as I am walking around the aisles, I see a tie rack. Yes, the grocery store is selling ties. I am sure that everyone reading this book has seen the same thing. I don't know about you, but I have never, ever stopped and even looked at one of these ties up close. Some of them, I must admit, have looked appealing from afar, but it would never occur to me that I could actually buy a tie of the quality I demand from a grocery store. In this example, the "you" blew it. The majority of people just don't buy ties at a grocery store. This would be like the hardware store selling deli pizzas and salami.

What is the lesson to be taken from this, then? If people are buying from you first, if you are at the forefront and in control of every sale, if all eyes are on you, doesn't it make sense to look, feel, and act like you are on stage every time you go into an appointment?

You have to make yourself the Home Depot in the above examples—the specialist of financial services. When people think of financial services, your name should pop into their heads. Do not be the grocery store unless you want to be thought of as the discounted day-old bread.

There are a lot of things in this world you can't control, but one thing is for certain: you can control the way you look, dress and act. Before you even step foot into any appointment, you must control yourself first. Once you have yourself under control, it only gets easier from there.

Chapter Five

Let's Talk About You

This chapter is the most personally sensitive chapter in this book. I want to point out that nobody, and I mean nobody, is perfect. This chapter is not meant to make anybody feel bad; it is meant to help you make more money. However, if after reading this chapter you feel a bit upset, that simply illustrates that this chapter had accomplished exactly what was intended, and that is to get you emotionally charged so that you take action to correct the problems. Did your parents ever tell you something that disturbed you

21

when you were a child, but they followed it up with, "I am telling you this because you are my child and I love you?" Well, I wrote this chapter because I care about everyone reading this book, and the truth of the matter is, I WANT YOU TO MAKE MORE MONEY!

How do you control yourself first? Another fact here which you must completely understand is that when you meet someone for the first time, they are going to look you up and down, whether you know it or not. They are going to make a judgment about you within the first five seconds. How does this translate for you? Either they will accept you, or they will have immediate reservations.

To make your sale much simpler, to make your life much easier, to make more money in your career, REMOVE THE POSSIBILITY OF THESE IMMEDIATE RESERVATIONS BEFORE YOU GET TO THE FRONT DOOR. Sound easy enough? Let's examine what I mean by that.

First of all, I try to conduct as many of my appointments as possible at the prospect's home until I make the actual sale and turn them into a client. I will outline the reasons for this in a later chapter. But the first thing you must do is to handle the reservations someone may have about your appearance before you even consider meeting with someone.

Facial hair is definitely out. While I believe that men should have no facial hair whatsoever, I don't want to alienate people out there who do. I will take it one more step and say that if you have facial hair, make sure it is well groomed. I was in a continuing education class not too long ago, and there was a salesman sitting next to me who had a very bushy mustache and goatee. It looked awful and was pitifully groomed. I am quite certain that in his initial five seconds with a prospect, his ugly goatee would cause an immediate reservation.

Next comes attire. I know it sounds simple to most, but there are a lot of salespeople out there who don't wear a suit when meeting a new prospect. The bottom line is a suit and tie for men, and a business suit for women. And guys, when you do wear a tie, make sure it is a clean one. Put down this book, walk over to your closet, and throw out the soup-stained ties right now! I'm not kidding; go and do it now! Also, while you're at it, get rid of the Disney character ties. Remember, you are a professional, not Donald Duck.

Speaking of ties, I remember not too long ago, a wholesaler told me something very funny, yet true. According to him, there is the short tie club and the long tie club. We sat and laughed about the people in the short tie club. And come to think of it, I have never seen someone in the short tie club who made a lot of money. Make sure you have your tie at the proper length. Be a part of the long tie club. This example alone illustrates how simple it is to control your appearance. Case in point–how difficult would it be to adjust your tie to be a bit longer if you are indeed a part of the short tie club?

Just as he coined this terminology to me when referencing ties, I came up with my own club to classify some salespeople. I call it the windbreaker club. Gentlemen, when you are wearing a coat and tie, do not, I repeat, do *not* wear a windbreaker. If it is cold or raining outside, wear the appropriate type of full-length trench coat or overcoat. The windbreaker club is reserved for used car salesmen. Remember, we are talking about investing life savings here, not selling Yugos.

Keep in mind that your prospects are looking at you and deciding whether or not you are worthy of investing their money for them. If you look sloppy, they will automatically assume that your office is sloppy. If you look disorganized, they will fear that your office is not organized. If you don't pay attention to details about yourself, the prospect will fear that their investments are going to be neglected as well. Don't do this to yourself. Don't lose a sale before you even have a chance to make one.

Hygiene is equally as important. Don't smoke cigarettes in your car on the way to your appointment, or right before someone comes to visit with you at your office. You may think you don't smell bad, but let me clue you in on something—you do! That two-minute puff on the way to your appointment isn't worth a lost sale. Also, be clean. White shirts with yellow stains around the cuffs or collars are absolutely inappropriate. I don't want to dwell much more on hygiene because this could get a little disturbing. You know who you are out there; just clean up because you will make more money by doing so.

Jewelry is part of your outer appearance. A wedding ring and a watch for the guys is all that is acceptable. Women, you can add a simple necklace and bracelet to this, but beyond that, do not wear any other jewelry. Also, men, get rid of the extra rings or bracelets. Again, this is all to overcome any immediate reservations by the prospect. I have some other jewelry I enjoy, but I wear it and enjoy it when my wife and I go out on a weekend. Remember, Monday through

Friday during business hours, it's show time and you are on stage. Do what it takes to make sales and money.

Last, how do you get to your prospect's home? Be careful what type of vehicle you are driving. Make sure it matches the type of prospects you are dealing with, and the market that you work in every day. Drive a respectable car. If your car has rust on it, get rid of it and get a new one. If you are driving a Mercedes Benz, you are surely going to raise eyebrows driving up to a depression era home. Don't kid yourself; you will be viewed differently from the get-go. This will translate into lost sales.

Let's end this chapter with some simple math. If you are truly committed to working in the senior market, if you really do want to make more money, is it worth it to drive a flashy car? Let's say you lose just one sale every two months due to the type of car you drive. Let's say it was, on average, a $50,000 annuity sale. (Remember, this is the tip of the iceberg. As we all know, there are always multiple sales in a home.) At a six-percent commission, this would be losing $3,000 every two months. Multiply this by six to determine the full year's loss, and that comes to an $18,000 loss for the year. This is all because of the car you drive. Is that Mercedes really worth an extra $18,000 a year to you?

Chapter Six

Your Office Team is Your Office Team

I have a small, but very effective staff running my office. It includes two valuable assistants. One of these women has the title of Office Team Manager. The other has the title of Marketing Team Manager.

My Office Team Manager does a wonderful job servicing client needs. She handles their requests for beneficiary changes, withdrawals, and many things of that nature. She also does a great job of processing and following up on my new business applications. Her voice is very pleasant on the phone and clients can tell when talking to her that she loves what she does. She is excellent at servicing the client's needs and keeping them happy when they call or stop in.

My Marketing Team Manager does exactly what she is supposed to be doing. First of all, she sets up seminars. Her job is to coordinate the seminar details from A to Z. She will then tell me when and where I have to be to make the presentations. She does this with meticulous precision. Her attention to detail is like no other person I have seen in this business and she helps me make a lot of money. She also arranges and monitors the marketing efforts as well as special events for clients, such as golf outings and Christmas parties. She is bar none, the best Marketing Team Manager any office could have.

So what is my job? My wife asked me the other day, "What do you actually do all day?" She always seems to call me when I am sitting at lunch with my cronies and having a good laugh. Nobody really had asked me that question before so bluntly. Without giving it a second thought, my immediate response was, "I am working with prospects and clients, and when I am not in appointments, I'm constantly thinking of new ways to make more appointments and see more people." My job is to talk to people and sell. I have the two well-qualified women cited above doing what they do best, so I can have all the time in the world I need to do what I do best. I have seen too many people in this business misuse their office team. What do I mean exactly? Well, the only misuse I am going to outline in this chapter is the most important one of them all. I have seen other professionals in our business who have their office team make their actual prospecting calls. This is undoubtedly a HUGE mistake! MAKE YOUR CALLS YOURSELF.

I know there are plenty of people in our business who make up every excuse possible why they don't have time to call their leads or do their prospecting personally. If this describes you, you must do one of two things. Either get over it and start making your calls yourself, or settle for making the money you're presently making without being able to step up to the next level. Why do I feel so strongly about this? The answer is simple.

As much as I appreciate my Office Team Manager and the job she does, as much as I feel my Marketing Team Manager is superior to others I have worked with in the past, they do not know half as much as I do about the psychology of the seniors I am prospecting, nor the products we sell. They have no clue how to combine these two things together in a telephone conversation with a senior and turn that phone call into an appointment. For every fifty calls they would make to get an appointment for me, I only have to make five. This is a complete waste of good prospects, which translates to a very large number of dollars being lost. Our office teams don't know how to engage these people in the type of conversation that leads to an appointment. And even if they are lucky enough to get the appointment for you, there is a very slim chance that the appointment was able to be qualified in any way whatsoever.

You are the financial services professional. You are the one with the training. You are the one with the licenses. You are the one who has been to countless classes to learn this stuff. You are the one who is learning to understand the way seniors think with their money. You are the one who has all the product knowledge. You are the one who has made successful sales in this business already. Who is reading this book right now to get better, you or your office manager? Leave the office work to the professionals you hired. These people know what their job is, and by executing their jobs effectively, they will make you more money. By wasting their valuable knowledge and time doing your prospecting, you will lose money. Make your own prospecting calls and you will make more money. That, you can take to the bank!

Chapter Seven

The Pre-Game Warm-up

As I mentioned earlier, I will always try to schedule the first appointment with a prospect at their home. When visiting someone at their home, they are more comfortable. You are talking to them in their domain, not yours. Think about it. If you are trying to get a first appointment with a prospect, and you ask them to bring in all of their mutual fund statements, IRA statements, brokerage account statements and their tax return, don't you think you might immediately scare some, if not most of them away? Yet, when you are in their homes, you can subtly ask for these things as the conversation permits, and yes, they will get up and get them for you almost every single time. The key to making this work however, is by turning their domain into your domain. If you really must see all of your prospects in your office, for whatever reasons, then this chapter and the next are not for you. You can go directly to chapter nine. However I do believe you are making a big mistake by not seeing people initially in their homes, which in turn, costs you money.

Every professional in our industry, and I mean everyone, should own a cell phone if they don't already. Just owning the cell phone isn't enough. Use the darn thing. What I am trying to say is that even if you are going to be five minutes late for an appointment, call the prospect from your cell phone and let them know that. It's just common courtesy, and it goes a long way. The last thing you want is to show up for the appointment, and have them question you as to why you were late. Also, have you ever been late somewhere before? How did the person react when you arrived? Almost always, they act polite, but you can tell they are a bit disgruntled. Take away the immediate reservation before it is even formed.

Before you even have a chance to sit down with a prospect in their home, you must first get there. You drive to the home and you pull up to the house and park your car. You should always park your car in the street if the environment permits it. You should never park in their driveway unless you absolutely have to. The last thing you want to happen in the middle of your appointment is for someone to ask you to move your car because they or someone else has to go somewhere. Or perhaps you have someone who is real finicky about his or her driveway. Even though you know your car is perfect, they may be thinking the whole time that your car is possibly dripping oil on their precious driveway. I had a guy in my old neighborhood who was out in his driveway every weekend scrubbing spots with soap and water. I kid you not. Do you want your prospect to be focusing on your appointment or the oil spot that isn't really happening? Remember to take away the immediate reservations before they are even formed.

Next, when you get out of the car, do not walk across their lawn, even that little strip of grass next to the curb where you park your car. Don't walk on that strip. There is almost certainly a small concrete walkway to step on to get to the sidewalk. Then use the proper walkway to get to the door. Some people are funny about their lawns. People go through great pains and expense to keep their lawns meticulous. They spend money on fertilizer and landscaping companies or more likely, they do it themselves. Nonetheless, it's not worth losing a sale to save a few feet in the walk from your car to the front door. Take away the immediate reservations before they are even formed.

Always go to the front door. Even if it is obvious to you that they don't use the front door, just go to it and let them tell you to go around to the side if they want you to. If there is a doorbell there, use it. Don't knock. If someone came to my house and knocked at the front door, my first thought would be, hmmm, is something wrong with my doorbell? Do you want your prospect to wonder about the doorbell, or to start thinking of the financial expert who is standing there waiting to be let in? I really don't know why this is so important, but that's exactly my point. What might not be important to me could very well be extremely important to someone else. Maybe not, but I am not about to risk losing a potential sale because I knocked instead of ringing. You must believe me when I tell you that these things really do matter, and they are so easy to do as long as you practice the little things and make them habitual.

So far, everything I've explained to you is a piece of cake. It matters and it works. However, the real fun begins when you enter the home. Now the game begins. Every home you walk into should be viewed as a treasure box. You never know what you will find. Sometimes you will find a treasure; other times you will find coal. The key is being able to walk out with the treasure whenever it is found. And by understanding what to do when you get into the house, you too can master the art of separating the gold from the silver.

Chapter Eight
The Red Carpet is All Rolled Out

You should now be at the point where your prospect has opened the front door to let you in. Keep something in mind at this point. No matter how they look, no matter how they act, they are happy to see you. Remember, they invited you to their home to visit them. It is now up to you to make your grand entrance and make sure that you don't do anything that will possibly take their minds off the sale. The red carpet is all rolled out and it's up to you not to muddy it up with your dirty shoes.

Just as there are immediate reservations that can be formed before you even get into the house, there may be even more that can be formed once you step through their door. Again, take away all of their immediate reservations. It is all a matter of being polite.

First and foremost is the handshake. A firm handshake is obvious, and not even worth talking about. Everyone knows that a milquetoast handshake will get you nowhere fast. The key, however, is this; don't always assume that someone wants to shake your hand. Not everyone feels comfortable shaking hands. Have you ever shaken someone's hand during an appointment and it was just the weakest, don't-touch-me handshake you have ever felt? I certainly have. In a situation like that, it was a mistake to extend my hand to make the shake.

So, how do you know? You must watch for the handshake signs. When looking in someone's eyes, see if those eyes wander down to look at your hand. This is a sure sign that they are waiting for you to extend the handshake. The other sign to watch for is someone's arm actually twitching a bit as if they wanted to shake your hand, but you haven't yet extended yours. I am not kidding. At the next appointment you walk into, see if this isn't true. You have to pay quick and close attention to this though, because it all happens very fast.

The next thing is your coat. If it happens to be cold or rainy and you are wearing a coat, it's time to take the coat off. A lot of people won't ask you if they can hang up your coat. It's going to be your decision what to do with it. Simply scope out a good spot for it, take your coat off, and ask politely if you can drape it over the chair or couch you have decided on. Don't put your coat anywhere without asking. Don't ask me why this is such a big deal, it just is. Take away any immediate reservations.

After the coat situation is settled, it's time to walk over to the kitchen table. Always, and I mean always let them lead the way. When you get to the table, immediately check out the layout of the room. Look for windows. If at all possible, try to make sure your prospect sits in a chair which will situate them with their backs to the window. The purpose of this positioning is that you don't want your prospect staring out the window, watching outside activities while you are speaking. However, make sure you ask if it's okay for you to sit down in the chair which you have chosen.

This is ever so important that you ask their permission. When they say yes, you must ask again, just to be sure. Why am I saying this? Think back to dinnertime with your family. Don't you and your family members sit in the same spot at the kitchen table night after night? For those of you whose kids have left home, when they do come home for the holidays or even just for a visit, don't they gravitate toward the same chair they were used to sitting in for a

43

good portion of their lives? The last thing you want to do is to sit in someone's chair. They will be thinking of the chair, rather than the financial services you want to sell them. Take away the immediate reservation.

I remember my days as a sales manager for a large insurance company where I personally recruited and trained a man who is a successful insurance agent to this day. Initially, he made all of the cardinal sins, but after listening to me and making the things he learned from me habitual, he corrected his oversights and now makes a comfortable living as an insurance agent. I remember one appointment where we were sitting at the kitchen table of a seventy-six-year-old lady. This particular insurance agent, still under my tutelage at the time, made a cardinal error while sitting at her kitchen table. The natural lighting in the room wasn't the best, so this agent took it upon himself to lean back in his chair, reach over his shoulder and turn on the lights. The moment he did that, I literally kicked him under the table. Think about his major error in judgment. Who did he think he was to give himself permission to use this woman's electricity?

This woman, like most of the people we deal with in the senior market, was a depression-era person. She grew up in the toughest of times. I am quite certain that the light in her kitchen was off because she wanted it to remain off to save money. Let's just say for one minute here that I am wrong—even though I'm not, but let's just say I am. This new agent still had no right to turn on the lights, regardless. Heck, he may as well have just waltzed over to the refrigerator and helped himself to the leftover casserole. This agent had a major strike against him before he even opened his mouth. Do you think it would have been appropriate for this agent to ask if he could turn the lights on instead of taking the liberty of doing it himself? The answer is absolutely, positively, no. Just to be polite, she might have said yes, but would then have been thinking of the kilowatts burning away instead of focusing on what we had to say. Take away the immediate reservations.

Last and ever so important, we can't neglect the briefcase. I have seen everything from plastic to tattered briefcases being carried by agents. I have also seen those ugly metal ones. Please, people—give me a break. I am embarrassed to even write about this, but here goes. The plastic ones should be used by your kids to carry their dolls and Hot Wheel cars. The tattered ones should be used at your home to store your old papers in, and the metal ones should be used by aluminum siding salesmen. Remember, you are a professional. Carry a nice leather briefcase. It should not cost more than eighty dollars at a discount office store for a presentable one.

When you are sitting at a kitchen table at a prospect's home, never, and I repeat, never put your briefcase on a table unless you ask permission first. I don't care how badly banged up the table may be, just don't do it. I ask every single time. There are a few instances when the prospect actually told me that they would appreciate it if I didn't put the briefcase on their table. Sometimes it is obvious that the table is very well cared for, and some type of fine grain wood. Other times, who knows, but it just doesn't matter. People can be strange sometimes. You don't want them to be thinking of the scratches you aren't really making, instead of focusing on what you have to say. Take away the immediate reservations.

If you master everything I mentioned above, if you try everything on a daily basis in your appointments, you will make more sales and you will make more money. Even if you forget the rest of what this book has to offer, which would be a costly mistake, and just be the guru of the grand entrance, you will make more sales and thus more money. The reason is simple. You will have mastered the art of turning their home into your domain. Their home is now your office, and they don't even know it. Conducting the actual business is getting closer and closer, and about to become a reality.

Chapter Nine

Never Judge a Book by Its Cover

Perhaps there are some of you who skipped chapters seven and eight and are rejoining us now. Welcome back. Regardless as to whether or not you see your initial appointment at your office or the prospect's home, the rest of the book now applies to you.

The title of this chapter has such a valuable lesson to be learned. I have some clients who appeared to have absolutely nothing, but in reality were millionaires. I always treat these people with the same respect and admiration as I treat all of my other clients. But only after eleven years in this business did it ever really hit home with me never to judge someone by the way they looked. I always felt that way, but I still did judge people. That is a crucial mistake that I will never make again.

I don't care how someone appears, if they will actually request my time to sit down and discuss my financial services with them, I will give them at least ten minutes to prove they are a prospect with an intention to buy. Why do I only give them ten minutes? The fact of the matter is that is all I give any prospect. You will learn about this in future chapters.

Luckily, when I was taught the old "book-by-its-cover" lesson, it didn't cost me any money. I actually made a lot of money. It happened like this:

My business associate and I do public seminars for people every single month. We ask the audience to fill out an evaluation card at the end of the seminar indicating whether or not they would like a complimentary consultation with one of us. At the end of the day, my associate and I equally divide up the cards we received, and we each go about our business of calling and scheduling our appointments. On one specific day, as we were dividing up the cards, one name stood out from the others because both of us vividly recalled this particular woman. We remembered her for bad reasons, not good ones. She was unkempt and a bit snooty. She looked as if she had never had her hair styled in her life, and her clothes were thirty years out of style.

I mentioned to my associate that he could have that card, because I didn't want it. We kind of joked around about it because neither of us wanted it to count toward our share of the piles we had divided in half. After all was said and done, I had agreed to take this woman's card and call her.

To make a long story short, I called this woman and scheduled an appointment with her. She had indicated that she wanted to bring her sister with her. I agreed. They didn't want me to come to their home, so they came to my office. The bottom line was that after ten minutes of talking to her, I discovered she had $400,000 in annuities out of their surrender periods and another $450,000 sitting in a money market bank account. I rolled over the complete $400,000 in annuities and made a lot of money doing it.

Not too long ago, my wife and I walked into a local furniture store. It was a hot summer night and I was wearing denim shorts and a t-shirt. I also had a baseball cap on. My wife was dressed for the climate and we had our nineteen-month-old daughter with us as well as our newborn. The salesperson asked us if she could show us anything and we said yes. I told her that we needed a kitchen table and would like to look at china cabinets. It is my belief that because of the way we appeared, the salesperson didn't take us seriously. What a huge mistake! I was good to go with my credit card, just aching to make a purchase. The mistake the salesperson made was not talking to us to discover why we needed a kitchen table. She showed us items for about five minutes, dismissed us as not being serious buyers, and went over to talk to another salesperson who was also doing nothing. If she would have asked a few simple questions, she would have discovered that my wife and I had just built a brand new home, and had moved in just two weeks previously. The kitchen table was just the tip of the iceberg. That was exactly the moment when I thought of this chapter for this book. Now granted, I wasn't a senior prospect for this salesperson, but everyone needs furniture, not just seniors. In fact just the opposite is probably true. People between thirty and sixty buy more furniture than seniors.

Because of these two valuable stories, I have made a lot more money. I will never judge people by their looks again. Everybody is deserving of ten minutes of my time—as long as they are senior citizens, of course.

Chapter Ten

Use Your Time Wisely

Whether you are in your office or at their home, use your time wisely. A first appointment should never last more than one hour. An hour-long first appointment is even pushing it, but I will give some of you the benefit of the doubt. I want to point something out. You are not paid to socialize.

The most important part of any sale is how you build the relationship with the prospect. And the most important part of retaining a client is to continually build on that relationship. This is not, however, synonymous with socializing. The only time it is appropriate to socialize is when you have turned the prospect into a client.

Whenever I conduct an initial appointment at my office, my colleagues will poke fun at me. They actually see me finishing the appointment in an average time of about half an hour. And the funny part about it is that if there is business to be had from these prospects in the future, I always get it.

You should be able to tell within the first ten minutes of your appointment whether or not the prospect is viable. Remember, if they have no intention of buying, they are no longer a prospect! Gracefully get them out of your office, or get up and politely leave their home so you can get back to doing things that make you money. Many times in my office, while sitting at the conference table with prospects, I have politely asked people to take their time and finish their coffee as I excused myself from the room. The appointment was over. I have no desire to continue to talk to them if they have no intention to buy.

You always have to do a five-minute warm-up. When you first sit with someone, what can you possibly talk about? You just met these people one minute ago. If you keep the following statement in mind, you will have no problem: everyone's favorite subject is himself. Just ask them for starters, "So which company did you retire from? How many years did you work there?" They can go on for at least five minutes just with those two questions. Now that you have them all warmed up, they are ready to move on to the purpose of the meeting.

The next thing you have to do is find out how much money they have and how their assets are currently invested. What I can't understand is why so many professionals in our business are afraid to ask people the details of how their money is invested. This is your work, and these people know that they are meeting with a financial services professional. Just ask them! You can say something such as, "I would like to start this meeting off by getting a list of assets down on paper. Do you currently own any mutual funds?" Then go on from there asking about stocks, annuities, life insurance, etc. You know the drill. This is commonly known in our business as doing a fact-find. On the rare occasion when they are unwilling to divulge this information, end the appointment gracefully and walk away. These people have no intention to buy and are no longer prospects.

Many people in our industry make as much, if not more than physicians. I am telling you this because I want you to equate your professionalism to a physician's. The minute someone puts "Dr." in front of a name, they immediately command respect from other people. Have you ever heard of someone going to a doctor, but refusing to divulge their medical history before the doctor starts diagnostic procedures? Of course not! That would be absurd. As a financial services professional, you should not continue on with any appointment unless you have obtained their investment history first. There is plenty of business out there for everyone, and more than enough people out there who want to do business with you. Make sure the prospects you are visiting with give our industry the same respect as any other professional would command, and if they don't, you will save yourself a lot of time. That will translate into more sales and money for you.

Chapter Eleven
Ask the Right Questions

So now you are sitting with the prospect and they have decided to give you the details on how their assets are currently invested. This is a major step in the right direction. But just because they have opened up their financial history to you, this doesn't mean they have the right to waste your time, nor should you allow them to.

You must start asking some feeler questions now. I call them feeler questions because they will give you the feeling of whether or not they will consider doing business with you. As you look at their financials, ask them flat-out if they are currently working with a broker. If their answer is yes, you haven't lost just yet, but you have to listen very carefully to their "yes" answer.

If they immediately answer yes, with the broker's name in the same breath, then you know they probably have a good relationship with that broker. Don't start packing your bags quite yet. Not everyone is happy with their current broker and that is exactly what you must ask them next. If they cite the fact that they have been working with the same person for twenty years, it's time to head for the door. Even if they aren't completely happy with the broker, chances are they will consult him or her before even considering doing business with you, and we all know that translates into a dead deal However, if they have been working with someone for a couple of years, but only know his or her first name, you have a pretty good shot at this and you should continue with your appointment.

I must stress to you again, don't waste time. Does what I explained above sound familiar to you? You can save yourself a lot of time and cut your losses. Remember, a prospect is no longer a prospect if they have no intention to buy. Don't feel as if you have to razzle-dazzle them with your charm and knowledge. The only people you have to razzle-dazzle with your charm and knowledge are the ones who are serious buyers. It is very easy to politely excuse yourself from the appointment. When was the last time you bumped into a person at the grocery store who was a prospect at one point but turned out to be a dud, and therefore you excused yourself? My point exactly—don't feel bad about ending the appointment if they are not serious buyers.

I remember in June 2001, I was sitting with a prospect at his kitchen table discussing the advantages of a fixed annuity for him. He appeared seriously interested. However, I made a cardinal mistake. I spent thirty minutes with him and that was twenty minutes too long. The mistake wasn't that I spent thirty minutes with him. I will get to the mistake later in the book. However, after twenty-eight minutes, he asked in his own words if it were possible to bypass me, the agent, and go directly to the insurance company to get the annuity, thus giving him a higher fixed rate by eliminating my commission. I decided he was worth two more minutes of my time to tell him how much of an idiot he was, and I got up and left his house as he was still sitting at his kitchen table wondering what had just happened. This yahoo had absolutely no intention of buying, so I left. Ninety-nine percent of the time, I leave politely and gracefully, but that other one percent of the time, I have to take a stance for all of the good people in our business and tell a guy like this to take a hike. Maybe he will think twice the next time before wasting someone else's time.

So, what was my mistake alluded to in the above story? It was a mistake that all of us have made, I guarantee you. The bright side of the story is that I will never repeat that mistake again, and because of that yahoo, I learned a valuable lesson, and have made even more money.

Chapter Twelve
Sit Back and Enjoy the Show

After you have asked your probing questions, it is time to listen. If you play your cards right, and if your prospect is a buyer, they will probably almost sell themselves. You just need to sit back and start taking a lot of notes. Even though you don't need to write down half of the things they say, it makes you look more interested.

People will start talking about how they don't like their current broker, or how dissatisfied they are with their investments. One of the most powerful questions you can ask someone is, "How do you feel about that?" Next time your prospect starts to complain about losing money in the markets or about the broker who doesn't pay any attention to them, ask them that very question. It will open up a flurry of emotions and conversation.

If you can get your client emotionally involved in what you are doing, you have won half the battle. But you must really listen and listen carefully. They will throw out buying signals. To give you an example, sometimes a client may ask if they can take their interest out on a monthly basis. My response to them is, "Would you prefer to take it out monthly?" They always answer with a "yes or some other solution to their own question. "Would you prefer to . . ." is such a powerful question. Inevitably it helps the prospects sell themselves.

Don't sit there for an hour and spew out too much information. You will probably leave the prospect confused, and thus lose the sale. I don't know about you, but I would much rather sit in an appointment for half an hour and listen, rather than sit for an hour and talk. By listening, I can ascertain whether or not this is a buyer. By being the talker, I would have no clue. There is no need to explain more than they will understand. It will be eating up more of your valuable time.

Next is body language. You have to watch this very carefully. I will give you a few examples in this book. Watch for the prospect to cross his or her arms together. If this is done, you know almost certainly that he or she is not interested. It is time for you to change course and try another avenue. My favorite form of body language is when the prospect starts to hold or scratch his or her chin. You now have a thinker, and someone who is seriously thinking of purchasing. There are so many other forms of body language to learn, but that is beyond the scope of this book.

By listening carefully and being able to read the body language, you will be in complete control. By sitting back and enjoying the show, you will be the one to decide when the show is over. You will not have to waste any more time listening to people drone on and on when they have no intention to buy from you. This will give you more time to save yourself for the main event, a serious buyer.

Chapter Thirteen
The Sole Purpose

The sole purpose of the first appointment is simply to get a second appointment, if you are able to qualify your prospect. The one thing you never, ever want to do is to try to make the sale on the first appointment. Even if you are unlucky enough to achieve this, it will rarely stick.

Why do I call you unlucky if you achieve this? Because you are going to go through all the steps, fill out all the paperwork, go home and high-five your spouse, have a nice dinner and feel good about yourself. How can that possibly be unlucky? Simply because, the next day when you walk in your office, you will have a message waiting for you, left for you by the client at 4:00 A.M., asking that you call them immediately. After all of the good feelings you had the day before, you are now about to get a big letdown.

When seniors sign over large amounts of their life savings, they have buyer's remorse like everyone else purchasing any other type of product. And if you didn't take the time to build the relationship and the sale properly, all of that hard work you did, albeit good work is going to go to waste. More often than not, when a senior signs papers on the first appointment, they aren't going to sleep that night. They will toss and turn, and stay up all night, wondering what they had done. That explains the voice mail message that was left for you at 4:00 A.M.

I will say it again. Never, ever have your prospect sign papers on the first appointment. It's kind of like going out on a first date. Take her out to eat, perhaps a nice dinner, maybe even a good-night kiss, but never tell her you want to start a relationship with her on the first date. She will dump you so fast that your head will spin. All you should be trying to do on your first date is get her to say yes to a second one.

All you should be doing on your first appointment is qualifying your prospect and then getting them to agree to a second appointment. There are very easy ways of doing this. Also, these easy ways will allow you to determine just how serious these prospects are and how much they trust you. The trust will be the key to possibly making the sale on the second appointment, or perhaps setting up a third after that.

Nonetheless, if you don't have the trust, pack up your briefcase and leave. Don't waste any more time because, for whatever reason, the trust just isn't there, and without trust, there will be no sale. The key test to see if there is any trust there is the way in which you leave your appointment. Papers in hand mean money in the bank.

Chapter Fourteen
Get the Statements

The last chapter touched on the subject of trust. There are many ways you can determine whether or not you have gained a prospect's trust. But in my opinion, there is only one best way. If they are a qualified buyer and if you are going to set up a second appointment, you need to walk out of that first meeting with their investment statements in your briefcase.

This may sound a bit intrusive, or difficult to do, but it is really quite easy. Once you have someone actually give you their investment papers to make copies of, you have just cleared a huge hurdle, and you are probably on your way to closing a sale either on the second appointment or for sure the third, if it takes that many. Think about what you would have accomplished. You would have persuaded someone who has known you for thirty minutes to hand over their personal information to you. So what is the best way to ask for these papers?

I always say to people, "Would you allow me to make photocopies of your statements so while I'm doing my homework for you, I won't have to scribble all over your originals?" Nine out of ten times, the prospect says yes. This is huge when they give these things to you. But you do have to follow up with one more quick statement before they have a chance to answer yes. Really quickly, follow up with, "I can do one of two things for you. I can either pop them back to you in tomorrow's mail, or I can just have them available for you at our next visit. Which would you prefer?" Did you notice how the "no" answer isn't even an option here? It works just about every single time.

When this appointment is over, feel good about yourself. You just did a great thing. However, you must keep one thing in mind. Always do what you say you are going to do. If you promised to mail the papers back the next day, then do it. Don't wait two or three days. Do it the next day at the very latest. Show this prospect that you are organized and on top of your game. Prove to them that you are the best in your business.

I have met too many salespeople who say one thing, but never follow through and do what they say they would do. These salespeople are always mediocre at best. The quickest way to screw up everything you just accomplished is by not doing what you said you would do. Don't go through all of this hard work, just to put yourself through another lost opportunity.

Now go back to your office and do your homework. If you get all the answers correct, the teacher will give you a nice fat paycheck at the next appointment.

Chapter Fifteen

Choose Your Words Carefully

You have been doing a great job so far. You just walked away from a first appointment situation with all of the prospect's account statements and a second meeting scheduled. It doesn't end here. You still have not made the sale, but you are almost there. Just be careful during the process as to how you phrase certain aspects of your conversation with the prospects.

You have to learn a new vocabulary. There are certain words you want to completely avoid. These words create negative feelings and perceptions in people's heads. You need to stay clear of these words and substitute a softer, kinder word. Let me give you a few examples, and I will try to emphasize the major ones. Keep in mind there are many more than I have room to write about in this book.

First and foremost is the word "appointment". People don't like to make appointments. When they make an appointment, they feel as if they are going to be committed to buying something from you. Substitute the word "visit." "Mr. Johnson, could I visit with you Tuesday at 1:00 or would Wednesday at 10:00 A.M. work better?"

Never tell anyone you are selling. People don't like to be sold. They do, however, like to be served. So instead of talking about the opportunity to sell them a product, how about rephrasing it? You would like to have the opportunity to serve them. McDonald's is an excellent example here. Years ago, their signs said millions sold. Then suddenly, when selling someone became politically incorrect, they changed all of their signs, to say billions served.

Another word to stay clear of is "buy." You could substitute the word "own." You don't want them to buy an annuity from you, but you would like to give them the opportunity to own an annuity.

A big no-no is the word "deal." If you say to someone they are getting a good deal, what do you think they would automatically think of? Exactly! They think of a car salesman. We'd all like to own a new car, but the process of actually purchasing one can be a nightmare. I do believe the word "opportunity" would be an acceptable substitution. "Mrs. Smith, owning this fixed annuity for your retirement needs would be a good opportunity for you." Some of you are now thinking about how corny that sounded. The only reason it sounds corny to you is because you are not used to saying things like that. To me, it comes second nature. Now substitute the words, "buying" and "deal" above. Sounds a bit like a Yugo car lot now doesn't it?

My favorite is the word "sign." I never ask anyone to sign an application. Rather I ask them simply, "Would you mind approving this?" as I point to the line where I want them to sign. Psychologically speaking, people are more comfortable when they are in control of their situations, and when you ask them for their approval, you just scored big points.

Don't say the word "contract" either. Whenever I deliver an annuity to a client, I refer to it as their certificate. A contract sounds too binding and can scare people away.

There are many more of course, but I think you get the point; plus, I mentioned the main ones above. If you just start with the words in this chapter, you will soon begin to recognize what I call "harsh" words on your own. Turn these harsh words into soft words and you will have an easier time getting people to sign on the dotted line. To reiterate from a previous chapter, it is of the utmost importance to remember that people buy from you first, the company second, and the product third. I think I have successfully taught you how to sell yourself so far, so the next challenge is selling the company. If you have grasped what I have taught you about selling yourself first, then the company is going to be a breeze. Let this next chapter serve as the breeze that will help you float over to your local bank to deposit a nice, big, fat paycheck.

Chapter Sixteen
The Company

Let's go over the correct sequence of the buying process again. People will buy from you first, the company second, and the product third. The majority of this book, so far, has been spent on the "you" part. It is only appropriate though, because it is you they are buying from first. If they don't like you, then you may just as well forget about telling them about any companies or products you represent.

Now that you have done such a good job getting people to like you very quickly, it is time to talk about the companies you represent. Perhaps you are an independent representative, or maybe you are a captive one. It doesn't matter. This part is all the same.

I don't know of too many captive companies left out there, and I don't want to name them in this book, because it seems that a lot of captive companies are leaning towards letting representatives write a bit more independently anyway. But the captive companies I am aware of are all big names in the business—names that most people recognize right off the bat. I started my career off as a captive agent for a very large, well known, respected insurance company.

As far as the independent representatives out there are concerned, you can pick and choose which company's products you want to promote, and those you don't. This is such a key issue, because you have the opportunity to introduce the company or companies you want to use with your clients in a very easy or an extremely difficult way. My question is who in the heck would want to make it difficult for themselves? The funny part about it is that I just wrote for almost fifteen chapters about the "you" part of the equation, and how to master it. I am only going to write in this one chapter about how to master the "company" part of the equation. That's how simple this is.

Has anybody reading this book figured it out yet? I gave you a bit of a clue when talking about the captive representatives being part of the big names in the business. That's right—only sell the companies that just about every Tom, Dick and Harry has heard of. You know which companies I'm talking about. I don't want to name them in this book, as there are far too many to mention.

But just think about it. If the prospect says, "What company do you plan on using for the annuity you are proposing?" and you mention some fly-by-night company that nobody has ever heard of, you have now put yourself in the position of having to spend another half-hour telling them about how great the company is, how wonderful the ratings are, how many years they have been in business, where there home office is . . . you all know the drill. We have all gone through that before. Why even put yourself through that? It's not at all necessary.

What I have learned over the years, and what I prefer to do is cut to the chase, mention a big name company that I know the prospect will recognize, and get on with the third part of the equation, the "product." With the specific companies I promote and write my business with, I never, ever get questioned as to how stable the company is, where they are located, how long they have been around, etc. Think about it this way. Why should you have to spend your time, energy, and money having to promote a company that has done a lousy job of promoting itself? What I mean is, if a company is not well-known and recognized by the average Joe, why make it your job to do their advertising? There are plenty of companies out there that spend millions of dollars each year to advertise and promote their organizations, to achieve name recognition. These are the companies you should be working with because simply put, it leaves you more time to talk about the more important subjects with your prospects.

This gives you plenty of time to talk about "product," and thus get to the signing of the application much, much faster. Also, it leaves very little room for losing the sale over the "company" part of the equation. The faster you can get to the "product," the more time you can actually spend on making the sale. This equates to many more sales, and thus more money. I want you to quit having to explain companies, so that you can talk about the things that really matter, which will in turn generate a much larger income for you.

Chapter Seventeen
The Product

Let's say it together one more time: you, the company, and last, the product. As the "company" part of the buying sequence only deserved one chapter, the "product" could have been dealt with in two or three sentences, but I will elaborate a bit more than just that. If I could get away with only saying one thing about the product, it would be this: sell concepts—not products. If you sell concepts to your prospects, they will buy the products, no questions asked. Let me explain a bit further.

85

You should not be talking to your prospects about annuities, life insurance, mutual funds, interest rates, etc. What you should be discussing with them is how these products can affect their lives, conceptually speaking, without yet mentioning the product itself.

You should be talking about burial costs, a surviving spouse having no money to live on, tax deferral, taxes, social security, prescription drug costs, housing costs, death, nursing home costs, investment risks, technology—the things that really matter to people. Talk to them about their kids, about their grandkids, or about their money. You should be talking about the things that your senior prospects talk about with their friends when they meet them for lunch, or at their local senior center for their weekly sheepshead game. Talk to them about things that will get them emotionally involved in what you are doing.

If you get your prospect emotionally involved, you will be completely in control of what happens next.

You will be one step closer to getting them to sign your application. I think this is so funny because I can't tell you how many times I have prospects signing applications and then asking questions later. I rarely discuss interest rates with prospects. Inevitably it happens, but only after they sign the application. They will look at me with a smile on their face and say something like, "By the way, what kind of interest will I be earning on that?" And then I answer them. I have never had someone say that the interest rate was too low.

I'm serious. I have actually had people ask me what my name was again, because they had forgotten it, but only after they had just signed over their life savings for me to invest for them. Can you believe that some of these people are investing their life savings with someone whose name they don't remember? Tell me they don't like me. They bought me first, the company second, and then the product, which really didn't matter to them much because they trusted me.

If you sell the concepts, the products will all fall into place. And if the products all fall into place, you will make more sales, and thus take home more money. Look at it this way. If all you did all day was talk about products, your job would be boring, and you would just end up confusing the heck out of people. If you confuse people, you will lose the sale. Talking about the concepts and the subjects that affect the senior prospect on a daily basis will not only create a more interesting conversation, but it won't confuse your prospect. And if your prospect is not confused, they are much more likely to sign your application.

The last thing any of us wants in this career is for our jobs to be boring. Talking about products is BORING. Try to picture this. You get home from work, sit at the kitchen table with your spouse, and your spouse says, "So, what did you talk about today honey?"

Would you like to answer, "I visited with three senior prospects today and we talked about annually stepped-up death benefits and mortality and expense charges." What a lousy dinner conversation. Or would you rather answer, "I had three senior prospects I visited today, and I actually helped them to lower their income taxes, provide for their grandchildren, and increase their standard of living, and honey, I'm not all that hungry tonight, because they insisted I try some homemade brownies that had just come out of the oven while I was there."

Have fun in this business. Don't make it more difficult than it already is. The more you simplify it, the more you talk to your prospects about the things that really do matter, the better off you will be. Make more money, and enjoy doing it.

Chapter Eighteen
From Prospect to Client

As you have read so far, I've always referred to the seniors as prospects. They will always be a prospect until you do one of two things—either by determining they are not a buyer, and thus moving on to the next prospect, or getting them to sign your application. Once they sign the application, they become a client. It is now time to ask them to sign, but you must be very careful. Sometimes seniors will sign today, but call you tomorrow and cancel. They sign because they are afraid to tell you no to your face. Let's now talk about how to maximize your retention of newly signed applications.

First of all, never ask them to sign. Remember chapter fifteen? You must use the word approve. It sounds silly, but it works.

Secondly, don't scare these people. Seniors have saved for fifty years to accumulate their wealth. They are not about to sign it all over to you at once. Be smart about this. Never, ever try to have them sign more than one transfer per appointment. If they have three different CDs and two mutual funds that you have in mind to transfer for them, don't talk about doing this all at once. Take it step by step. When someone has five or ten different accounts, as soon as I get one account, I know darn well that in due time, I will have all the money under my management, even if another broker is working with some of the other accounts.

The key to this is to go after the least threatening piece of money first. Many times this will translate to the smallest account they have, but who cares? Don't get greedy, because if you try to transfer everything at once, you will end up with nothing. A lot of little crumbs make the cake. If you follow this very important advice, not only can you have the cake, but you can eat it too.

There is another important aspect which applies to transferring their bank accounts (CDs, money markets) to whatever investment you are recommending. I have seen so many brokers make this mistake, and it has cost them money more often than not. If your client approves the form for transferring their CD from the bank, don't send this form through the normal channels. You MUST personally take this form to the bank, walk it up to the teller, provide proper identification, and politely say, "Hello, I would like to close this account out for my client. Here is the signed authorization form, and please make the check out to ABC Company." I have never, and I repeat, never walked out of a bank without the check. After I have the check in hand, I then send it either to my broker dealer or the fixed annuity insurance company in accordance with compliance.

What did this effectively accomplish? It doesn't give the bank officer any chance whatsoever to call the client and talk them out of the transaction. The fun part about this is when the bank president actually comes out to see what you are doing. The president will give you a look that seems to say, *Damn, I can't really do anything about this*. Then they try to act a bit presidential in front of their teller. I always like to introduce myself to them with a handshake, and give them my own look. Feel good about yourself when you do this. It's quite an accomplishment. And always answer them with your look that says, *I just made more money in one day than you will make all week*. Smile, be confident, and be happy that you didn't lose the sale due to the bank representative calling your client.

You have now turned your prospect into a client, but it's not over yet. You have gone through a lot of work to get to this point with your new client, but it can all be unraveled very quickly if you don't achieve a smooth transition from what the client had been used to doing for years, to what they just trusted you to do for them. Remember, just because they approved the application, doesn't mean you get paid yet. The money still has to come in, and this can take weeks, sometimes months, depending on the type of transfer you are doing. A lot can happen in the span of a few weeks, and certainly anything can happen over a couple of months. Do the proper follow-up work, and the next check you will be transferring will be your commission from the mailbox to your bank account.

Chapter Nineteen

More Important Than the Sale

Too many representatives out there think that once the prospect has signed on the dotted line, and has become a client, the sale is complete. This kind of thought process could be the kiss of death to the entire sale. What you do after the sale is just as important as everything you did to lead up to the sale.

You've put so much time and energy into the process up to this point, it would be a shame to lose it now. So what should a representative do after the sale?

95

First, let me point out once again that the senior mind thinks much differently than a thirty-year-old. A thirty-year-old may, for example, have $5,000 to invest if they're lucky. However, a senior probably just invested ten to twenty times that at a very minimum. When seniors make changes to their money, they don't sleep the night after they signed.

You have to take care of questions in their heads before the question becomes a problem. Here is what I do. Without exception, I always call my senior client the morning after I make the sale. I usually make up an excuse as to why I am calling. I say something like, "Good morning, Mr. Smith. I was just calling because I wanted to verify your date of birth before I send your paperwork in to be processed. I would hate to get it wrong, and it's easier to correct now rather than later."

When asking a question like this you will get one of two responses. The first could be simply that they give you their date of birth, and then they thank you once again for helping them. This is exactly the answer you want. It pretty much translates into the fact that they had a good night's sleep and they don't have any questions at this point.

The second type of response would be, "I am glad you called. I was thinking this whole thing over and I had a question about blah, blah, blah." Did you notice they didn't give you the date of birth yet? This is a serious concern of theirs and you should now answer their question over the telephone and reassure them about their investment decision. Now ask again for their date of birth, get it from them, and tell them you are sorry to have bothered them. They will say, "No problem whatsoever," and say goodbye. Whether you know it or not, you just saved the whole sale.

You must understand that I have absolute confidence in my sales abilities. Making that follow-up call the morning after is all part of the sale. It has nothing to do with a poorly done job on the part of the salesperson. You are the financial services professional; these are your products and you understand them inside and out. There is no way your client, senior or not, is going to remember everything you told them. What you effectively did by calling the next morning was to remove what I call the "Uncle Ernie factor." What is the "Uncle Ernie factor," you ask?

Everybody has an Uncle Ernie in the family. This is someone who knows everything about absolutely nothing. The last person you want your client to be talking to is Uncle Ernie. Once Uncle Ernie gets his two cents in, your sale is completely gone. Uncle Ernie can be a daughter, son, lawyer, accountant, brother or sister, just about anyone other than you. I have never run into an Uncle Ernie however, who was a fully licensed representative in the financial services industry. It's actually amazing how all your years of experience, or for those of you new in the business, all the classes and education that led you to completing your licensing, can suddenly be completely compromised by someone who doesn't know squat about what we do for a living.

It usually goes something like this, "My daughter called me this morning, and she works for this doctor, you know, who has done quite well in the market, and she told me to hold off on things for awhile until she can arrange for me to talk to her boss about all this." I swear, I have heard things like that before and it is so aggravating. First of all, the daughter doesn't even know enough to figure out that the doctor doesn't want to talk to her seventy-eight-year-old mother unless it is about an angioplasty. Secondly, it's all a bunch of smoke, and an excuse to begin with.

Please don't let this happen to you. One telephone call after the sale can save you a lot of money and aggravation!

Also, do frequent follow-ups after the sale. As mentioned before, I have a full-time office manager in my office, and she spends a great deal of her workday following up on new business—not just with the companies, but with the client as well. Don't do this all yourself. It is very time-consuming. A lot of times, even though you fill out the proper transfer forms, the company you are transferring the funds from may require their own forms be filled out. This adds extra time to the transfer process.

Or perhaps, and we all have done this from time to time, you forget to check a box on a transfer form, or on the application. This will also delay things, and sometimes considerably. Do you really think that if you forgot to check a box on the transfer form, the company who is losing the business is going to call you and tell you? "Hello, is this John Smith at ABC Financial? We just wanted to give you a call and let you know that you forgot to check box 8a, and if you would please do this and fax it over to us, we will send out the $250,000 check right away." NO WAY! It is your responsibility to follow up on the paperwork. The faster the money transfers, the less time your client has to talk to other "know-it-alls" in the family.

We all know that a transfer can sometimes take two months to complete, especially if the other company is trying to conserve the business. As I mentioned in a previous chapter, a lot can happen in two weeks, let alone two months. Call your client frequently during this period of time just to check up on them. Have your office manager, or whoever does your follow-up work also call your client frequently to keep them up to date on the process. A lot of representatives think just the opposite, that they shouldn't call for fear of bothering or worrying the client. Put yourself in the client's shoes for a moment. You just signed over a quarter of a million dollars, and three weeks go by with nothing to show for it yet. That would make anyone nervous.

Frequent follow-up is the key to retaining the sale you worked so hard for. Not only is it great for retaining the sale, it also builds the relationship that you have started with your client, even stronger. Every time you make a new client, you should have one major goal in mind—to build a relationship so strong, that when Uncle Ernie approaches that client sometime down the road, your client tells Uncle Ernie to buzz off. Once this is accomplished, you only have one more problem. What happens one year down the road when your client gets a cold call from another broker promising the moon and the stars, and the client decides to meet with that broker? If you don't think it will happen, you're wrong. It will. And it can be any one of your clients, even the ones you would least expect.

Chapter Twenty

Have Another Drink, and Another

Everything you just learned by reading this book is key to being able to make money and survive in this business. But what I am about to tell you in this chapter is how to make even more money in this business.

My business is better than ever, but it has taken twelve years to build it to this level. I also strongly feel that even though I have achieved top-of-the-table stature within the insurance industry, I still have not hit

103

my peak. The reasons why I feel this way are as follows:

I have only been in the business for twelve years. We all know people who have been in this business for twenty or even thirty-plus years. As it turns out, I currently derive at least half of my current income from my existing client base. The other half comes from prospecting and the referral business. If I double my client base over the next twelve years, I will be making a heck of a lot more money just from my clientele alone. Why am I telling you this? If I don't take care of my clients, they will leave me. And likewise, if you don't take care of yours, they will find someone (or someone will find them) who will.

You must be able to offer your clients exemplary service. When they call you and you aren't there, you must get back to them that same day. If they call in at the end of the day, you must call them back no later than the following morning. I have heard other people say that as a rule of thumb, you should get back to people within twenty-four hours. I think the people who live by that rule are crazy. Twenty-four hours is a long time. Think about it. If you were to call your accountant at 9:00 A.M. with an important question, and the office manager said he or she wasn't in but that you would be called back, wouldn't you get a bit perturbed, once 4:00 P.M. rolled around and you still had no return phone call? These clients like you, and trust you immensely. You must make them feel individually like they are your most important clients. Here is my rule of thumb. If you have a cell phone, USE IT! Return your client's calls from your car. Turn off the radio talk shows with people calling in the middle of the day who have nothing better to do, and use your cell phone to make money.

You also have to keep in mind that what may seem trivial to you is important to the client. If your client calls in to make a beneficiary change, get it done immediately. It is important to them to have it done, so do it. And don't wait a week to do it either. Client service is what your office manager should be doing on a daily basis.

Another biggie is the gatekeeper theory. Every big executive seems to have a gatekeeper answering the telephone. Read this and read this very carefully. YOU ARE NOT A BIG EXECUTIVE! You are salesperson. Your job is to be accessible to your clients and make sure they get the service they deserve. You should never screen your telephone calls from your clients. Every call that comes in the office for you, you should personally take, or call back if you happen to be busy. It is just one more chance for you to talk to your clients without having to call them first. You should carefully listen to their service request, and politely explain to them that you will be informing your office manager of the type of service they need, and that your office manager will be calling them back to make the necessary arrangements. The last thing you want is for your client to feel as if you are only personally accessible when you want their money.

Seniors love the fact that they can talk to you personally at any time. They have enormous respect for you as a businessperson, but don't let that respect turn into resentment by making them feel as if they can't reach you personally. I can't tell you how many comments I get from my senior clients telling me how happy they are because I can always be reached. This is one of the huge things that separates me from a lot of other people in our business.

In the introduction of this book, I told you that you could go back and drink from the same well over and over again. Keep this in mind. These senior clients were saving their money for fifty years before they met you. Just because you met them and followed my strategies and were able to get control of every dime, doesn't mean they suddenly quit saving! They've lived their whole lives as savers, and they will die as savers. Call them frequently, keep in touch, and visit with them at least twice a year. They will always have more money for you. Cheers!

If you are in front of these people as frequently as I'm telling you to be, there is no way another broker will ever break the relationship you have established, even if the other broker does get into their home. I've had many clients meet with other brokers. Their reaction was to call me immediately afterwards, tell me what they had learned, and ask me if there is anything else they should be doing. I even have a client who sends me mail on a regular basis—literature they've gotten from other seminars, prospecting mail they receive, and newspaper clippings from other brokers' advertisements. This is a relationship, and this is trust. These people will never take their business elsewhere. I am their broker.

Chapter Twenty-one
How I Knew

Let's go back and re-examine chapter one. I mentioned specifically near the end of chapter one that after Sylvester the Sales Manager walked through the front door of my client Karl's home, I knew instantly that the sale was mine. Why?

I purposely showed up early for the appointment to help strengthen my relationship with Karl, not to talk about fixed annuities. We talked about his family, his childhood, and many other pleasant subjects other than business.

The first mistake young Susie made was to show up at someone's home without telling the prospect that she was bringing a manager with her. Afterward, Karl mentioned to me that he felt a bit "double-teamed," so to speak.

I learned that was happening due to my very important, routine follow-up call after the client had signed on the dotted line. Had I not made this call, I am quite sure it would have been too late to save the sale. Who knows what Susie and Sylvester the Sales Manager would have said to the client had I not been in the room. The fact of the matter is that the information they dished out when I was there was totally incorrect due to a lack of product knowledge on their parts. But, had I not been there, my client Karl would have probably believed them.

Secondly, when I went to the front door to greet Susie and Sylvester the Sales Manager, remember how I mentioned that my eyes suddenly lit up? Why? Well, immediately my attention was diverted to the shiny, white BMW parked out front. Now, had I been in a ritzy part of town, this would have been fine, but we were in a very modest, blue-collar, humble neighborhood. This was perfect as my client noticed the same thing I did, and we actually laughed about it after Sylvester the Sales Manager left. In fact, in the middle of Sylvester's pitch to my client, I actually directed the conversation to focus on his BMW, and he was dumb enough to start talking about the new Mercedes he was waiting to trade his BMW in for. I almost started laughing right then and there.

We were dealing with an eighty-seven-year-old man who lived through the depression—a man who wouldn't turn the air conditioning on during a ninety-degree heat wave. This was a man who had bought his son a used bike for Christmas fifty years earlier. (His son told me all about it.) How dare anyone flaunt their expensive material goods in front of this man and think for one moment they would get away with it.

After I peeled my eyes off the BMW, my focus shifted to Sylvester the Sales Manager himself. First of all, he wasn't wearing his suit coat. I knew it was hot outside, but when you are going for $100,000 plus, look completely professional, not partially. Secondly, Sylvester the Sales Manager weighed at least three hundred pounds. Truly! Appearance is very important, but forget the sale and the money. This guy has to lose weight just so he will be able to see his forty-fifth birthday. I think you get the point about this.

Susie did well by convincing Karl to allow her to come over, but due to my diligence and my normal follow-up techniques, she didn't get very far. The next part of the appointment was the mere formality of going through the motions at the kitchen table. Susie and Sylvester the Sales Manager had already lost the sale before they ever sat down at the kitchen table.

Their product knowledge was horrific, and none of their facts were straight. Susie might have won a small battle, but the bottom line was, I won the war. Not only did I make a lot of money over the next few months getting Karl to transfer all of his investment assets to my company, but I also made a dear friend.

Chapter Twenty-two
The Best Salesperson You Know

So, who is the best salesperson you know? Take a few minutes and really think hard about this question. I wish I could be sitting with everyone reading this book right now to hear your answer.

The answer should be you! The best salesman I know is myself. You need to display confidence with every single prospect you have. You have to let people feel they are working with the best person in the industry. Don't feel inferior to anyone out there. I remember one time I took a client away from another local financial services representative who has his own Saturday morning radio show. Just because he is on the radio doesn't make him the best in this business. For that particular client, I was obviously better.

As I do public speaking at my estate planning seminars, I actually tell people that when they sign up for their free consultation, they are going to be meeting with some of the best people in the industry. When I am in an appointment at someone's home, I will tell him that I am amongst the best people they can possibly work with in the state of Wisconsin. And the greatest part about all of this is that I truly mean it.

You have to be careful though. There is a fine line to be drawn between confidence and arrogance. Telling your prospects once that you are the best is a beautiful display of confidence. Telling them more than once is an ugly display of arrogance. I know of one particular representative who happens to be one of the most arrogant individuals I have ever met in my life. Other people I know feel the same way about this person. His arrogance shines right through him and people can sense it. They are repelled by it, BIG TIME. Is that the kind of reputation you want?

If you are confident, your clients will see it in you. Successful people prefer to do business with other successful people. Confidence will translate into more business.

I want you to feel like you are the best salesperson in the world. I always tell other representatives, if I had to go to the local car dealership and sell cars for a living, I would sell more cars than anyone on the lot, even the veteran salespeople. If I had to work at a clothing store, I would sell more clothes to people than anyone who has ever worked there before. I hope you understand by now that it has nothing to do with the product you are selling, but everything to do with you and your performance!

Now that you are done with this book, I want you to go out and make more money. I want you to feel good about yourself. I want you to display a feeling of confidence like none other. I want you to go out there and find all the prospects who are clients of the representatives who are doing it the wrong way, and make them yours. I want you to build a wall of relationships around your clients that no other broker can climb. Arrogance will take you absolutely nowhere, but confidence will drive you straight to the bank.

Anthony Raad

About the Author

Anthony Raad is a graduate of the University of Wisconsin. He belongs to the National Association of Insurance and Financial Advisors as well as the National Institute of Certified Estate Planners. He holds membership in and is a graduate of the Life Underwriter Training Council Fellows. He has been awarded the Top of the Table status in the Million Dollar Round Table. He is the founder and president of Lincoln Financial Services in Brookfield, Wisconsin. He is a certified estate planner and a renowned public speaker. Anthony is an avid tennis player and would never turn down an invitation to golf.